D1557918

McNay Art Museum
An Introduction

theMcNay

McNay Art Museum
in association with
Scala Publishers

Contents

◄ **Raoul Dufy**
French, 1877–1953
Golfe Juan (detail), 1927
Oil on canvas mounted on panel,
32³/₁₆ x 39⁵/₈ in.
Bequest of Marion Koogler McNay
© 2010 Artists Rights Society (ARS),
New York / ADAGP, Paris

Foreword

For many years, visitors to the McNay Art Museum have asked for a brief guide. The opening of the Jane and Arthur Stieren Center for Exhibitions in 2008, which doubled the size of the museum, has made such a publication a necessity. The addition of the Stieren Center's twenty-first-century design to a 1920s gem of the Spanish Colonial Revival style makes the museum's architecture a destination in itself. Moreover, this expansion allows us to show all aspects of our superb collection as well as special exhibitions as never before.

McNay Art Museum: An Introduction provides a window into the museum's rich collections, its architecture, its programs, and the story of how one woman's vision led to the founding of the first museum of modern art in Texas. I hope it will serve not only as a guide to visiting but also as a remembrance of the unique combination of art and architecture in a beautiful garden setting at the McNay.

The growth of the museum's collection, which has almost doubled over the past two decades to nearly 20,000 works of art, is a tribute to Marion Koogler McNay. Her founding bequest of some 700 works acts as a magnet for generous gifts by others and as an inspiration to generations of museum staff and board members to strengthen and expand the collection by strategic purchases. A community-based, private institution, the McNay has become one of the most distinctive museums of modern art in the United States and a great legacy to the people of San Antonio and south Texas.

William J. Chiego
Director

◀ **Edward Hopper**
American, 1882–1967
Corn Hill (Truro, Cape Cod)
(detail), 1930
Oil on canvas, 28½ x 42½ in.
Mary and Sylvan Lang
Collection

Introducing Marion

First-time museum visitors often ask, "Who was McNay?" The McNay Art Museum's founder, at one time or another, answered to Jessie Koogler, Marion Koogler, Mrs. McNay, Mrs. Atkinson, and Mother Marion. Indelible in the museum's history, however, is the name Marion Koogler McNay, which she used during her last years. Her passion for art began early in life and led her to become an art educator. Later her family inheritance enabled her to build a Spanish Colonial Revival-style mansion and assemble a remarkable group of European paintings, American drawings, and Southwest objects. In her final decade, she generously assisted student artists by sharing her collection and residence, resolving to leave both to establish the first museum of modern art in Texas. The story of Marion's life continues to intrigue new McNay visitors, as well as long-time supporters.

The only child of Clara (Lippincott) and Dr. Marion A. Koogler, Jessie Marion Koogler was born in 1883, in DeGraff, Ohio, and was apparently named for an aunt and for her father. Only a year after Jessie's birth, Dr. Koogler accepted a position as a physician for the Santa Fe Railroad, moving the family to El Dorado, Kansas. There, Jessie spent her childhood years. When she was ten, her family traveled to see the World's Columbian Exposition in Chicago, where the art and architecture no doubt stimulated her curiosity. Jessie's first intensive study of art occurred in fall 1900, at age seventeen, when she enrolled in the Fine Arts School at the University of Kansas in Lawrence—some 120 miles from the watchful eyes of her parents.

In 1903, when she matriculated in the School of the Art Institute of Chicago (SAIC), Jessie began using her middle name, Marion. Marion Koogler attended classes at SAIC from fall 1903 through spring 1905. Attachments to Chicago, its Art Institute, and friends she made there continued throughout Marion's life, ending with a stipulation in her will that the director of the Art Institute should approve any new acquisitions for the McNay, a formality since legally rescinded.

Marion returned to SAIC art classes from fall 1911 through spring 1913. As a single woman in her late twenties, she lived on Indiana Avenue only a short walk from the Art Institute and Lake Michigan. In those years she began doing medical illustrations for eminent surgeon, Dr. John Benjamin Murphy. When Marion's father retired in 1912, her parents moved from Kansas to the central Ohio town of Marion in Logan County.

◀ Marion Koogler (McNay) Atkinson, 1932

Marion sent to her parents and to Don's mother this "finished while you wait" photographic postcard, taken on their honeymoon in Columbus, Ohio, 1917. The newlyweds stand next to a palm plant and in front of a seaside backdrop. Don is dressed in his army uniform with slouch hat and boots. Marion wears a stylish plush suit with fur collar and cuffs. As 1917 fashion prescribed, her hat, with its crushable, high crown, nearly covers her hair; a plumed ornament adorns the front.

The following year, on March 24, the Art Institute of Chicago opened the *International Exhibition of Modern Art,* also known as the 1913 Armory Show in New York City. SAIC students burned in effigy the artists Constantin Brancusi and Henri Matisse during the twenty-three days of the Armory Show in Chicago. But for Marion Koogler, seeing Impressionist, Post-Impressionist, Fauvist, and Cubist works by modern Europeans surely generated thoughts of creating and owning similar art. In 1914, Marion joined her parents in Ohio, accepting a position as substitute art supervisor for the Marion City Schools. A letter of recommendation from the school board's superintendent described her as "one of the best qualified art teachers I have ever known … she arouses and develops the child's observation and enlarges his aesthetic nature." As Marion shared her love of art with the children of central Ohio, the Kooglers learned of the 1915 major oil strike on land they had purchased in El Dorado, Kansas. As a consequence, the family's resources expanded greatly. Marion's trip to New York City in 1916 included a visit to the Anderson Galleries, where she saw modern American paintings by John Marin and William Zorach, whose works she would one day own.

By December of 1916, Marion had formed a friendship with the young station manager for a streetcar line, the Columbus, Delaware & Marion Railway Company. At twenty-three, Don Denton McNay described himself in a letter: "I ain't much of a fellow to put my feelings into words, but in my silent sort of way, I want you to know that I am awful glad that you will be home in less than a week, time never went so slow as the past few weeks have." Marion was visiting a "Miss [Harriet] Hurst" in Chicago when she received the letter. Don promised to pick her up when the Chicago train pulled in and to "do the heavy work." In late 1917, after the United States had officially entered World War I, Don enlisted in the U.S. army. On December 9, Marion and Don married, both giving their ages falsely as twenty-eight on their marriage certificate.

Sergeant and Mrs. Don McNay then left Ohio for his military training in Laredo, Texas. When Don was deployed to Jacksonville, Florida, they stayed at the Menger Hotel in San Antonio before he departed. Marion then returned to Ohio. In Florida, Don developed the influenza that swept the country in 1918, so Marion traveled to be with him. She returned to Ohio a widow. Only ten months after their marriage, Don Denton McNay died on October 25, 1918.

Marion Koogler McNay remained in her parents' residence in Ohio even after her second marriage in January 1921, to Charles Newton Phillips, a banking friend of her father. In the summer of 1921, Dr. Koogler died. While Marion had assumed the role of society matron with determination, even purchasing land in Florida and Ohio with her husband, the Phillips marriage was not a happy one. Marion and her mother, Clara Koogler, traveled to Florida and Texas. In time, Marion engaged her father's attorney to file for a divorce. Mother and daughter returned to Marion, Ohio, in February 1926, for the dedication of a new Skinner pipe organ at the First Presbyterian Church in memory of Dr. Marion A. Koogler.

On February 8, 1926, Marion Koogler Phillips opened a bank account in San Antonio, Texas, where she brought her mother, possibly revisiting happy memories of Don McNay and their days in south Texas. A letter dated March from the Ohio attorney indicates a resolution of the divorce from Charles Phillips. Marion was then free to remarry and she lost no time in doing so. On May 18, 1926, she wed Donald Taylor Atkinson, a renowned eye surgeon who evidently was impressed with her experience as a medical illustrator.

Dr. Atkinson owned acreage northeast of downtown San Antonio, an area called Sunset Hills. In January 1927, architect Atlee B. Ayres wrote to Mrs. Atkinson asking that he and his son Robert M. Ayres be considered for designing the Atkinson residence. By early September excavation began for the new structure. The death

Inscribed "Christmas 1926" on the back, this snapshot of Marion and Donald Atkinson was taken before their Spanish Colonial Revival-style residence at Sunset Hills was started.

of her mother that year dimmed Marion's enthusiasm. Nevertheless, during the thirty-two months of construction, Marion kept a close watch over every detail, even requesting that the stucco on the outside surface be completely redone with more texture. In August 1929, the Atkinsons issued final payment for the house to Atlee B. and Robert M. Ayres. Plans for a formal opening of the Sunset Hills mansion in June 1930 progressed despite the October 1929 stock market crash. Photographs and newspaper accounts of the party, as well as of the 1932 wedding of Marion's cousin, clearly show that Marion and Donald Atkinson entertained in a generous and elaborate fashion. Marion returned to painting watercolors, in addition to doing some medical illustrations for her husband's books.

In the late 1920s Marion began to collect art seriously. Her first major purchase was an oil painting by Diego Rivera (p. 35), who visited San Antonio in 1927 when the Witte Museum exhibited some of his paintings. Gallery catalogues in the McNay's archives indicate that Marion bought watercolors by Mary Cassatt, George Grosz, and Paul Signac on several trips to Chicago. She befriended Edith Halpert, owner of New York's Downtown Gallery, and welcomed Halpert's advice on art acquisitions. In 1934,

◀ Marion Koogler
McNay with Paul
Gauguin's *Portrait of
the Artist with the Idol*
(ca. 1893), ca. 1942.

Marion met Los Angeles art dealers Ruth and Dalzell Hatfield in New Mexico.
They visited Sunset Hills and Dalzell advised her on purchasing such works as
Marc Chagall's *Dream Village* (1929) (p. 18) and Paul Gauguin's *Portrait of the Artist
with the Idol* (ca. 1893). In September, Marion traveled to Chicago for A Century of
Progress International Exposition and saw Vincent van Gogh's *Women Crossing the
Fields* (1890). A month later she purchased the van Gogh from the Chester Johnson
Galleries in Chicago.

On regular summer excursions to Santa Fe and Taos, New Mexican jewelry,
pottery, *santos*, and textiles entered Marion's collection. But as her passion for
art advanced, her relationship with her husband declined. In their 1936 divorce
agreement, Marion retained the Sunset Hills mansion, her art collection, and
twenty-three acres of land surrounding the house. She also requested permission
to return to the name "Marion Koogler McNay."

Two subsequent marriages temporarily deprived her of the McNay name. In
1937, she married Taos artist Victor Higgins. Only a year younger than Marion,
Indiana-born Higgins had also studied at the Art Institute of Chicago before going
on to Paris and Munich. In March 1940, the union of the magnanimous Texas heiress
and the impoverished painter ended bitterly. Six months later Marion wed Adelbert
E. Quest, whom she had known from her dealings with the Johnson Galleries in

Chicago. In May 1941, Marion McNay Quest accepted an invitation to serve on the board of the Museum School of Art, which conducted art classes at the Witte Museum. In August that year, the Quests divorced.

In 1942 when the conditions of World War II prevented the Witte from holding art classes, Marion McNay offered to build an art school on her property and eventually to give her house for a future gallery. Throughout the 1940s, minutes of the board meetings indicate that the art school's success depended greatly on Marion Koogler McNay's unceasing largesse. She opened the patio for classes; built a studio classroom and library; allowed students to study her art collection; paid for supplies, salaries, exhibitions, catalogues, parties, and newspaper advertisements; and even housed out-of-town instructors. In 1949, talented art student Carlos Rios attended the School of the Art Institute of Chicago paid for entirely by "Mother Marion", as she signed some of her letters and telegrams to him.

Marion McNay's last public appearance was at the annual students Christmas party on December 22, 1949, when she came down from her sick bed to enjoy Santa Claus giving presents to every guest. She died on April 12, 1950, of a heart condition and pneumonia, with antecedent conditions of diabetes and a fractured disk. Marion Koogler McNay's will stipulated that her art collection and residence become an art museum. On November 4, 1954, with John Palmer Leeper as its first director, the McNay opened its doors with an exhibition devoted to Pablo Picasso.

▼ At this annual Christmas party for students (ca. 1946), art dealer Dalzell Hatfield stands behind Mrs. McNay, shaking hands with Santa in the entrance hall of the McNay residence.

The McNay Residence in 1929

In the 1920s and 1930s, affluent San Antonians showed an intense interest in the combined Anglo and Hispanic heritage of the region. Renowned San Antonio architects Atlee B. Ayres and his son Robert complied with and expanded this interest by designing more than fifty houses, located in suburban neighborhoods north of downtown, in their distinctly Spanish Colonial Revival style. Still gracing northern neighborhoods are the light stucco outside walls, colorful Mexican tile insets, elaborate wrought iron grilles, and red tile roofs of the Ayres and Ayres style. Robert M. Ayres explained that the southern climate of the United States afforded designers opportunities for including vine-covered open terraces, loggias, balconies, sleeping porches, and open-air dining spaces, all banked with a great variety of flowers and shrubs. In addition, the architects arranged rooms in their Spanish Colonial Revival designs to capture prevailing summer breezes, with bedrooms on the southeast side of the house.

On January 1, 1927—about nine months after Marion (McNay) and Donald T. Atkinson married—Atlee Ayres wrote a letter to Marion offering to design a house to her requirements. When the Atkinsons hired the firm in July of that year, Ayres and Ayres planned the largest and the best of their Spanish Colonial Revival-style residences. Built on farmland that Donald Atkinson owned, the property appeared on plat maps as "Sunset Hills." Indeed the house sits on a hill with a breathtaking view of the sunset. As the work progressed on the Atkinson house, Atlee Ayres and his wife took frequent trips, such as one to California, that generated suggestions for Arts and Crafts tile companies to supply decorative features in the house. Their son Robert remained in San Antonio to deal with Marion's demands for the Sunset Hills mansion. During the spring and summer of 1928, Robert Ayres wrote to his father, away in Europe, about his frustration with the project:

> Mrs. Atkinson was out the other day for the first time and looked at the plastering on the inside and stucco on the outside of the house and it has put her back to bed and she is not up yet. She said she wanted it much rougher than it was, in fact she would not accept the house unless it was rougher so [the contractor] has agreed to do over the inside and outside to her satisfaction.*

Apparently, Marion changed the color schemes often during that summer.

Designed in a U-shape around a central patio, the Atkinson house did indeed include loggias, balconies, sleeping porches, and open-air dining spaces, all banked with flowers and shrubs. Ayres and Ayres also arranged rooms to capture summer

▲ Called "LIBRARY" on the Ayres and Ayres 1927 plan for the house, this room featured built-in bookcases and a double-sided fireplace on the common wall with the central patio. The bookcases and the inside fireplace were removed when the house became an art museum in the early 1950s.

*Correspondence, April 14, 1928. The Ayres and Ayres collection, The Alexander Architectural Archive, The University of Texas Libraries, The University of Texas at Austin.

▶ The dining room table is set for the wedding of Marion's cousin Jessie Lippincott to Eugene Winkworth on October 26, 1932. Diego Rivera's *Delfina Flores* (p. 35) hangs on the far wall.

▼ The entrance hall showing the double staircase and doors to the patio with gates by San Antonio craftsman Theodore Voss. Wrought iron features throughout the house were made by Voss.

breezes inside and out in the central courtyard. A typical atrium in a Mediterranean residence, enclosed within and completely surrounded by the building, features a pool in the center and protects from the sun and hot air. The patio's east end was enclosed by a stucco wall, which the museum replaced in the 1970s with new gallery spaces. In the middle, a pool with several fountains and sides lined with pressed concrete tiles in a variety of colors echoes the Baroque shape of a window at Mission San José in San Antonio. Several vibrantly colored Talavera tile murals, probably from Puebla, Mexico, adorn surfaces in the patio. Above a south wall open-air fireplace, Don Quixote astride Rosinante and Sancho Panza appear in a large tile composition; other patio walls have small square tiles depicting incidents from Miguel Cervantes's seventeenth-century novel. An impressive peacock panel,

in brilliant blue, yellow, and white Talavera tiles, holds a prominent place on the north wall of the patio.

On the south side of the patio, a wooden sleeping porch—once so necessary in the American South—cantilevers from the second floor, where the owner's apartment with bath and dressing room, as well as a guest room and bath, were located. A staircase with tiled risers, possibly a sampler of tiles produced by the California studio of Harry Hicks, leads to a door that gave access to the owner's apartment and to an upper open terrace. The sound of rippling water, the swaying of palm trees, the magnificent hues of bougainvillea and other foliage combined with the wrought iron gates, lanterns, and furniture as well as the tiled surfaces, make the patio an enchanted place for parties, both in the 1920s and today.

Marion reportedly created the hand-stenciled patterns on the Roman arches and the creatures on the ceiling coffers and beams. In the entrance hall, arches supported by Corinthian columns frame the door and bay windows, forming cross vaults. At Atlee Ayres's urging, the Atkinsons selected Arts and Crafts tiles by Ernest Batchelder of Pasadena, California, for the floors of the main rooms and on the indoor stair risers. Small relief tiles of animals or abstract patterns in subtle color glazes punctuate the larger flat tiles.

French doors at the north and south sides of the rooms opened to the patio or outside terraces, cooling the house in an era before air conditioning. After the formal opening of the house on June 10, 1930, a reporter from the *San Antonio Evening News* described the dining room as "the peacock dining room," no doubt because peacocks dominated its décor. Peacocks adorned a tapestry on the north wall and drapery at the French doors. Stenciled on the coffered ceiling are peacocks and cranes. A stylized peacock's tail forms when the iron gates into the room—now moved to the center opening on the west wall—are closed. Also, Marion was reputed to have live peacocks roaming the grounds.

Construction, at a cost of nearly $140,000 for the house alone, took sixteen months, with completion in September 1929. Another $100,000 was paid for landscaped terraces and the interior patio garden.

The McNay is grateful to architectural historian Stephanie Hetos Cocke for sharing her research on Ayres and Ayres, Architects. Her unpublished paper "The Spanish Residential Architecture of Atlee B. and Robert M. Ayres" is the source for much of the information on pages 12–14.

How the
Museum
Expanded

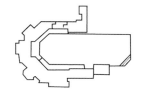

1954

Following Marion Koogler McNay's death in 1950, renovation of her residence begins, as well as hiring of the first director, John Palmer Leeper. The museum officially opens on November 4, 1954.

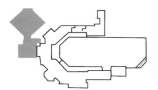

1970

The Emily Wells Brown Sculpture Pavilion and Gallery open. The Brown Gallery functions as the McNay's first facility for public programs.

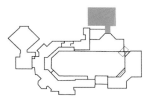

1973

The Mary and Sylvan Lang Galleries open. The Langs bequeath their collection of European and American early twentieth-century Modernist work in 1975.

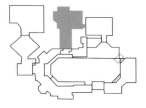

1975

The Jack and Adele Frost Galleries open, completing the circle of galleries surrounding the McNay's central patio.

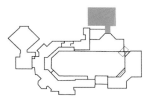

1982

The Jerry Lawson Print Gallery, the first space dedicated to showing works on paper and incorporating a Print Study Room, opens, through the generosity of Lawson's mother, Mrs. Gus Glasscock.

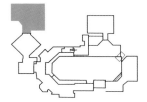

1984

The Tobin Wing, housing Robert L. B. Tobin's theatre arts collection and the McNay's art reference library, opens through the generosity of his mother, Margaret Batts Tobin.

1987

The Stieren Wing for art storage and receiving is completed, the gift of Jane and Arthur Stieren.

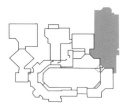

1993

The Blanche and John Palmer Leeper Auditorium opens, providing space for social events, lectures, concerts, and video screenings.

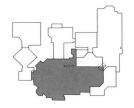

2001

Marion Koogler McNay's house is restored and renovated, providing new gallery space as well as a central plant for heating, ventilation, and air conditioning.

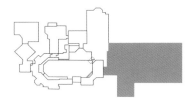

2008

The Jane and Arthur Stieren Center for Exhibitions opens, providing 7,500 square feet of dedicated exhibition space, a 2,500-square-foot sculpture gallery, and an outdoor sculpture garden.

Jane & Arthur Stieren Center for Exhibitions

When the McNay opened the Jane and Arthur Stieren Center for Exhibitions in 2008, the museum's dynamic special exhibitions program expanded and twentieth-century sculpture in the collection gained new spaces, both inside and out. Designed by internationally renowned architect Jean-Paul Viguier, the Stieren Center includes a flexible space for major exhibitions as well as for smaller focused installations. A grand indoor sculpture gallery overlooks an acre of outdoor sculpture gardens. In addition, the building houses the Museum Store, the Elizabeth and William J. Chiego Lecture Hall, and the Valero Learning Centers.

▲ Entrance to the Stieren Center for Exhibitions with a view of the glass curtain wall that looks out on the sculpture garden

▼ Tobin Exhibition Galleries in the Stieren Center during *American Art Since 1945: In a New Light*, summer 2008

Library and Archives

A noncirculating fine arts research facility since the museum's founding in 1954, the McNay Art Museum Library serves museum staff, docents, and visitors. Built on the core collection of Marion Koogler McNay's personal library, the museum library includes more than 30,000 volumes, 28,000 vertical files, and other significant holdings.

A unique strength of the library is its connection to the museum's collection, sharing a focus on modern and contemporary European and American art, as well as theatre-related publications. In addition, the library collects materials that support research for exhibitions, and maintains the museum's archives and records in the Stieren Center's specially designed facility, with compact shelving and cold storage for preserving photographs.

▲ McNay Art Museum Library

▲ Elizabeth and William J. Chiego Lecture Hall

▼ Families enjoying an art activity in Valero Learning Centers

Education

Central to the McNay's education programs are tours for adult and student groups, conducted by volunteer docents since 1964. Other educational events include public gallery presentations by curators, scholars, and musicians. Concerts and small theatrical performances are offered in Leeper Auditorium, with its superb acoustics for instrumentalists and vocalists. Lectures, panel discussions, and films are presented in Chiego Lecture Hall, with its handsome pearwood paneling, stadium seating, digital projection system, and surround sound. Workshops for teachers, teens, and families, as well as screenings of videos on artists, take place in Valero Learning Centers.

European Art
1800s–early 1900s

Marion Koogler McNay's superb group of French Post-Impressionist and School of Paris works forms the heart of the museum's painting collection of the nineteenth and early twentieth centuries. Her love of bold form and color, as well as a taste for unfinished works and paintings that show the artist's hand, appears in many of these works. Since her founding bequest, the painting collection has grown to represent Impressionism and its forerunners, as well as later European works.

Pre-Impressionist paintings show the development of plein-air painting in France. Beginning in the 1820s with slices of nature by Robert-Léopold Leprince and Jean-Charles Rémond, the collection continues with mid-century Barbizon painters and related landscape artists. Narcisse-Virgile Diaz de la Peña and Jean-Baptiste-Camille Corot, as well as Realism's standard-bearer, Gustave Courbet, all demonstrate their own take on nature, both real and imagined. Eugène Boudin, who painted the McNay's atmospheric harbor scene at Trouville (1871), taught Claude Monet to paint out-of-doors, which led directly to Impressionism.

Paintings by Édouard Manet, Camille Pissarro, Pierre-Auguste Renoir, and Alfred Sisley—whose *The Road from Saint Germain to Marly* (1872) appeared in the first Impressionist exhibition in 1874—represent the Impressionist masters. Pissarro's *Haymakers Resting* (1891) (front and back cover), influenced by Georges Seurat's pointillism, was part of New York's great Havemeyer collection before Mrs. McNay acquired it. Her Renoir, *Gabrielle in Oriental Costume* (1913), is one of six in the McNay collection, ranging from an 1880s sketch of the Isle of Guernsey coast to *Serenade* (1919). The Impressionist group culminates in Monet's great *Nympheas (Water Lilies)* (ca. 1916–19), from the collection of Margaret Batts Tobin.

Daring stylistic experiments by Post-Impressionists Paul Cézanne, Gauguin, and van Gogh epitomize Mrs. McNay's attraction to vibrant color, dynamic form, and unfinished works. Her preferences also embraced School of Paris works by Chagall, Matisse, Amedeo Modigliani, and Chaim Soutine. Matisse's brilliant color in *The Red Blouse* (1936) parallels three works by Raoul Dufy, especially his *Golfe Juan* (1927) (p. 2). The transitional Picasso collage *Guitar and Wine Glass* (1912) establishes the foundation for later Cubist paintings by Georges Braque and Fernand Léger. Other donors added works by the Nabis painters Pierre Bonnard and Edouard Vuillard.

Mary Cassatt

During the winter of 1890–91, the American expatriate Mary Cassatt created a print suite of ten color aquatints in Paris. The suite is Cassatt's masterpiece and one of the landmarks in printmaking history. The artist intricately combines delicate drypoint lines and subtle colors applied with separate aquatint plates. The flattening of surfaces, overall patterning, and skewed perspectives in Cassatt's prints are indications of *Japonisme*, the influence of Japanese art in France at the end of the nineteenth century. Even the subject matter of each print, women going about their everyday domestic chores, is derived from Japanese art, especially the color woodblock prints that Cassatt collected. Through the generosity of donor Margaret Batts Tobin, the McNay is one of a handful of museums in the world to own the complete suite of Cassatt aquatints.

▶ **Mary Cassatt**
American, 1845–1926
The Letter, ca. 1890–91
Drypoint and aquatint,
plate 13 ⅝ x 8 ⅞ in.
Gift of Margaret Batts Tobin

The McNay collection also includes a Cubist-influenced collage and paintings by the Russian Natalia Gontcharova; German Expressionist paintings by Alexey von Jawlensky, Ernst Ludwig Kirchner and Gabriele Münter; a rare night scene by the Dutch Piet Mondrian; and German Bauhaus period works by Grosz and Paul Klee.

Acquired after the museum opened, European sculpture corresponds to the painting collection's strength in French artists and now represents key sculptors and movements of the nineteenth and early twentieth centuries. Three artists of the Romantic period established the editioning of bronzes in the early nineteenth century: Antoine-Louis Barye, David d'Angers, and Jean-Jacques Feuchère.

▶ **Alfred Sisley**
British, 1839–1899
La Route de Saint-Germain à Marly (The Road from Saint Germain to Marly), 1872
Oil on canvas, 18¼ x 24 in.
Gift of Dr. and Mrs. Frederic G. Oppenheimer

◀ **Eugène Boudin**
French, 1824–1898
Trouville, 1880
Oil on canvas, 21¼ x 29¼ in.
Museum purchase in part
with the Helen and Everett H.
Jones Purchase Fund and the
Ralph A. Anderson Jr.
Memorial Fund, with
additional funds from
Charline and Red McCombs
and, by exchange, from the
bequest of Gloria and Dan
Oppenheimer, Mrs. Robert
Wesselhoeft Jr., and the
Louise C. Clemens Trust

► **Henri Muller**
Manufactured by
Muller Frères
Lunéville, France
Bats Vase, ca. 1900
Double overlaid, etched,
and wheel-carved glass,
9¼ in. high
Jeanne and Irving
Mathews Collection
of Art Glass

▼ **Claude Monet**
French, 1840–1926
Nympheas (Water Lilies),
ca. 1916–19
Oil on canvas, 51¼ x 78¾ in.
Collection of The Tobin
Theatre Arts Fund

▲ **Paul Cézanne**
French, 1839–1906
Houses on the Hill,
1900–1906
Oil on canvas, 25 3/8 x 31 3/8 in.
Bequest of
Marion Koogler McNay

▶ **Paul Gauguin**
French, 1848–1903
Sister of Charity, 1902
Oil on canvas, 25¾ x 30 in.
Bequest of
Marion Koogler McNay

The next generation of late nineteenth-century sculptors, including Jean-Baptiste Carpeaux, Albert-Ernest Carrier-Belleuse—Auguste Rodin's teacher—and Aimé-Jules Dalou, brought greater naturalness and movement into sculpture, inspired by Baroque and Rococo works. They led the way to Rodin, with whom nineteenth-century sculpture culminated, and experiments of the twentieth century began.

Rodin's mastery of motion and distortion of the human form emerged in works such as the *Burghers of Calais* (late 1890s). Following in Rodin's path were early twentieth-century sculptors such as Antoine Bourdelle and Jacob Epstein. Those who took a different direction include Aristide Maillol with the classical repose of *La Nymphe* (1930) and Belgian sculptor George Minne's anti-heroic *Man with a Watersack* (1899).

▲ **Auguste Rodin**
French, 1840–1917
Five studies for the *Burghers of Calais*, late 1890s
Bronze, ranging from 15 15/16 in. high to 18 5/8 in. high
Museum purchase and gift of the Tobin Foundation

▲ **Ernst Ludwig Kirchner**
German, 1880–1938
Portrait of Hans Frisch,
ca. 1907
Oil on canvas, 44¾ x 44¾ in.
Museum purchase

Pablo Picasso

In her bequest, Mrs. McNay gave the museum two important works by Pablo Picasso: the oil painting *Woman with a Plumed Hat* (1901) and the collage *Guitar and Wine Glass* (1912). Each represents a critical moment in the artist's development. The nineteen-year-old artist painted *Woman with a Plumed Hat* while he was still in Madrid in 1901. Later that year, in Paris, Picasso painted melancholy figures with blue dominating the compositions. Many scholars consider some of his Madrid paintings, such as the McNay's early oil, as the beginning of his Blue Period. The 1912 collage marks a short period that year when Picasso and Braque both experimented with wallpaper, newspaper, oilcloth, and other materials to add various textures and colors to their Cubist compositions. From these collages, the synthetic phase of Cubism evolved with artists doing faux paintings of these colorful materials, as in the McNay's still lifes by Braque.

As a gift of the Estate of Tom Slick, the McNay received Picasso's beloved *Portrait of Sylvette* (1954), a late painting with similarities to his analytic Cubist works. With the bequest of Jeanne Lang Mathews, two more oils joined the collection, including *Femme couché sur la plage (Woman Lying on the Beach)* (1932), one of a series of miniature variations on Picasso's great erotic nudes of that year, a high point in his career.

Picasso was a prodigious printmaker and the McNay owns more than seventy of his prints, as well as a drawing, a watercolor, sculptures, ceramics, and a theatre maquette, bringing the museum's collection of works by Picasso to more than ninety.

◀ **Pablo Picasso**
Spanish, 1881–1973
Guitar and Wine Glass, 1912
Collage and charcoal on
board, 18⅞ x 14¾ in.
Bequest of
Marion Koogler McNay
© 2010 Estate of Pablo
Picasso / Artists Rights
Society (ARS), New York

▶ **Pablo Picasso**
Spanish, 1881–1973
*Woman with a Plumed
Hat*, 1901
Oil on canvas, 18⅜ x 15⅛ in.
Bequest of
Marion Koogler McNay
© 2010 Estate of Pablo
Picasso / Artists Rights
Society (ARS), New York

American Art
1900–World War II

In the decade after the museum opened, director John Leeper developed a major strength in paintings by artists of the Stieglitz group, named for legendary American art dealer Alfred Stieglitz who promoted the careers of American Modernists. Abandoning imitative realism for the theories of Wassily Kandinsky and Arthur Wesley Dow, many of these artists expressed personal feelings or interpreted nature through harmonious arrangements of color, line, and other formal elements.

Influenced by the flat decorative patterns and primary colors of German folk art and Native American works, Marsden Hartley focused on military pageantry in *Portrait Arrangement* (1914), painted during his time in Germany as World War I was about to erupt. Russian-born Max Weber, whose diverse painting styles are represented in three paintings at the McNay, spent time in Europe absorbing both Fauvist and Cubist influences, as demonstrated by his colorful collage-like oil *Conversation* (1919). Marin's loosely painted views of New Mexico mountains and the Maine sea coast allow the imagination to fill in areas of blank paper or canvas. Two paintings by Arthur Dove maintain a typical landscape format while abstracting visual realities into compositions of color and shape. Dove's *The Brothers* (1942) invites metaphorical interpretations unless one sees his ten watercolor studies, which the McNay owns. His architectural starting point of houses inhabited by a monastic order evolved into a flattened geometric tour de force. Georgia O'Keeffe's *Evening Star No. V* (1917) marks the period of Stieglitz's initial interest in the work of the indomitable artist who became his wife.

Along with the Stieglitz circle of artists, their contemporaries—calling themselves the Eight—and other Modernists also found a home at the McNay. Without representing the grittiness that earned the group the nickname Ashcan School, the McNay's paintings do reflect the American experience. Ernest Lawson's gray winter day in an urban harbor contrasts with William Glackens's summerhouse scene, which shows an admiration for the painting style of Renoir. Maurice Prendergast's experiences in Italy similarly trace their origins directly back to French Post-Impressionist brushwork techniques. Arthur B. Davies's small abstraction of a bird chirping, from around 1915, and Zorach's *Milking Time (Echo Farm, New Hampshire)* (1917) seem to draw from Kandinsky's theories on sound and color, as did the Stieglitz artists.

◀ **Max Weber**
American, born Russia,
1881–1961
Conversation (detail), 1919
Oil on canvas, 42 x 32 in.
Museum purchase

While the world struggled with harsh economic realities, American artists represented the lives of ordinary people. Rivera's *Delfina Flores* (1927) is one of his numerous depictions of a domestic worker's daughter. In 1929 Rivera began painting murals in the Palacio de Bellas Artes in Mexico City. In the 1930s he took on several projects in the United States at a time when many American artists were hired by the Works Progress Administration to paint murals in public buildings throughout the country. Many of these painters became well known after World War II. Among them is Ben Shahn, who frequently produced images of social or historical commentary, such as his *Sing Sorrow* (1946) representing Americans' grief over Franklin Delano Roosevelt's death.

A favorite work at the McNay is Edward Hopper's *Corn Hill (Truro, Cape Cod)* (1930) (p. 4). Hopper and his wife spent several summers on Cape Cod. In the painting, cirrus clouds spread across the sky, leaving deep shadows on the green hillside and the houses. Sunlight on the sand and ocean side of the buildings clearly defines the forms and conveys the solitude and respite of a location now overrun by summer tourists.

▲ **Arthur Dove**
American, 1880–1946
The Brothers, 1942
Tempera and wax emulsion
on canvas, 20 x 28 in.
Gift of Robert L. B. Tobin
through the Friends
of the McNay
© The Estate of
Arthur G. Dove

▲ **Marsden Hartley**
American, 1877–1943
Portrait Arrangement, 1914
Oil on canvas, 39 3/8 x 32 in.
Museum purchase

Georgia O'Keeffe

From 1916 through 1918, Georgia O'Keeffe held teaching positions in Canyon and Amarillo, Texas, and corresponded during those years with friends in New York, including Stieglitz. In 1918, while she was recuperating from flu with friends near San Antonio, Stieglitz sent photographer Paul Strand to San Antonio to take her back to New York by train.

No fewer than five works by O'Keeffe are in the McNay collection. The early watercolor, *Evening Star No. V* (1917), and a later, large oil, *From the Plains I* (1953), relate to the artist's statement that "Texas is my spiritual home." The watercolor is one of ten such images that she painted while teaching at West Texas State Normal College in Canyon. *From the Plains I*, a gift of the Estate of Tom Slick, recalls O'Keeffe's time in Amarillo. Close-up views of natural objects, one of O'Keeffe's favorite approaches, are the focus of *Leaf Motif #2* (1924), *Pink and Yellow Hollyhocks* (1952), and *Goat's Head* (1957), giving the McNay a wide range of the artist's work.

▲ **Georgia O'Keeffe**
American, 1887–1986, *Evening Star No. V*, 1917
Watercolor on paper, 8 5/8 x 11 5/8 in.
Bequest of Helen Miller Jones
© 2010 Georgia O'Keeffe Museum / Artists Rights Society (ARS), New York

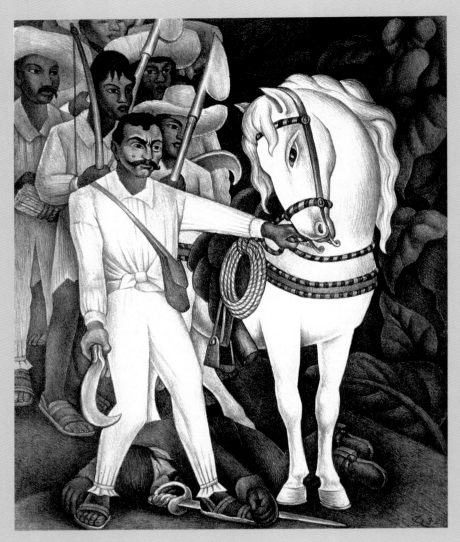

Mexican Prints

The McNay's longstanding commitment to Mexican art began with Mrs. McNay's acquisition of an oil painting by Diego Rivera, *Delfina Flores* (1927), which she bought the year it was painted. Also, director John Leeper had a strong interest in Mexican printmaking and acquired key works by *Los Tres Grandes*: Rivera, José Clemente Orozco, and David Alfaro Siqueiros. The McNay has all but one of the lithographs that Rivera made, including his masterpiece, *Zapata* (1932), a portrait of the great revolutionary and land reform champion. Rivera depicts Zapata as a noble hero of the Mexican Revolution, standing over a vanquished soldier and dressed in the simple cotton clothes and sandals of a Mexican fieldworker.

A fine group of prints from the Taller de Gráfica Popular (TGP), one of the most influential print workshops of the twentieth century, includes outstanding works by Leopoldo Méndez, a founder of the TGP, as well as rare lithographs by Francisco Dosamantes and Jésus Escobedo.

The McNay has one of the most important collections of Mexican prints in the United States or Mexico and is recognized nationally for its exhibitions and publications of this material. Of particular note is an exhibition co-organized with the Philadelphia Museum of Art titled *Mexico and Modern Printmaking: A Revolution in the Graphic Arts, 1920–1950* (2006–07).

▲ **Diego Rivera**
Mexican, 1886–1957
Zapata, 1932
Lithograph,
image 16⅛ x 13⅛ in.
Museum purchase with funds
from the Cullen Foundation,
the Friends of the McNay,
Charles Butt, Margaret Pace
Willson, and Jane and
Arthur Stieren
© 2010 Banco de México Diego
Rivera Frida Kahlo Museums
Trust, México, D.F. / Artists
Rights Society (ARS), New York

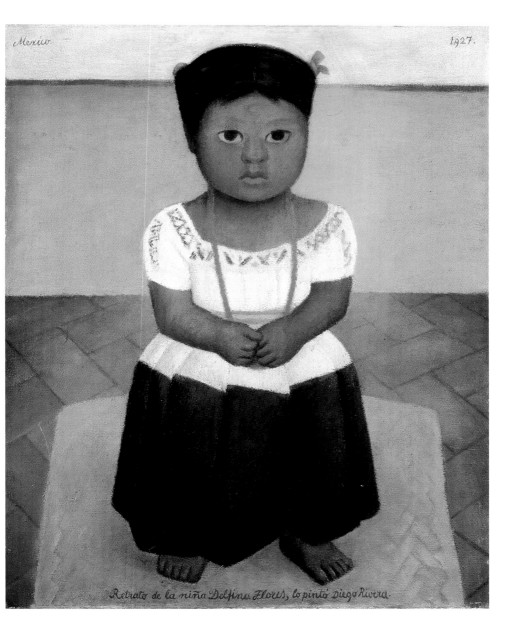

Mexico.   1,927.

Retrato de la niña Delfina Flores, lo pintó Diego Rivera.

Art after World War II

American and European postwar paintings and sculptures at the McNay reflect two parallel developments in the art world: an ongoing departure from illusionism while maintaining references to nature; and the dominance of the abstract or nonrepresentational.

Paintings that include the human form range from Picasso's late monochromatic, geometric images of women and Jean Dubuffet's expressive and highly textured figures, to Robert Indiana's homage to Marilyn Monroe. A still life by Ben Nicholson and Charles Sheeler's elegant architectural composition illustrate further alternatives to the prevalence of nonrepresentational painting after the war.

As the art world's focus shifted from Europe to New York City, an explosion of large abstract painting occurred during the period, influenced by émigré European abstract and surrealist artists along with American painters' experiences creating murals. Postwar Abstract Expressionism in the museum's collection includes intimate drip paintings by the legendary Jackson Pollock, an early canvas by William Baziotes, two brooding works by Theodoros Stamos, a large gestural painting by Friedel Dzubas, and Willem de Kooning's ostensibly abstract transfer painting of a nude on newspaper. Grace Hartigan is represented by two major pictures and Joan Mitchell in three varied canvases. Compositions by Larry Rivers show him abandoning the purely nonrepresentational, introducing people and spaces in his pre-Pop paintings. Paul Feeley's 1960s abstractions revel in rich stained color concealing the artist's hand.

Growth in the area of postwar sculpture began after the museum's opening in the mid-1950s and increased in the 1990s. The Stieren Center's sculpture galleries now provide ample room for exhibiting Alexander Calder's *Four Winds,* Seymour Lipton's *Moloch #3,* and David Smith's stainless steel drawing in space, as well as Isamu Noguchi's painted aluminum creation; Richard Stankiewicz's assemblage of found objects; and works by Raoul Hague, Ibram Lassaw, and Reuben Nakian. Several examples by British artists Barbara Hepworth and Henry Moore, along with an organic abstract figure by Jean Arp, allude to the human form. More directly figural are Germaine Richier's elongated standing woman, Zorach's mask-like head, and a dramatic portrait by Alberto Giacometti from his *Annette* series (1962–65).

◀ **Joan Mitchell**
American, 1926–1992
Hudson River Day Line
(detail), 1955
Oil on canvas, 79 x 83 in.
Museum purchase with
funds from the Tobin
Foundation
© The Joan Mitchell
Foundation

A small figurative assemblage by Jim Love and numerous examples by Expressionist Charles Umlauf enhance the collection with works by two artists who were active in Texas.

Major outdoor objects, including monumental examples by Tony Smith and Alexander Liberman, transform the McNay's grounds into a sculpture park, now augmented by the new Brown Foundation Sculpture Terrace and gardens of the Stieren Center for Exhibitions.

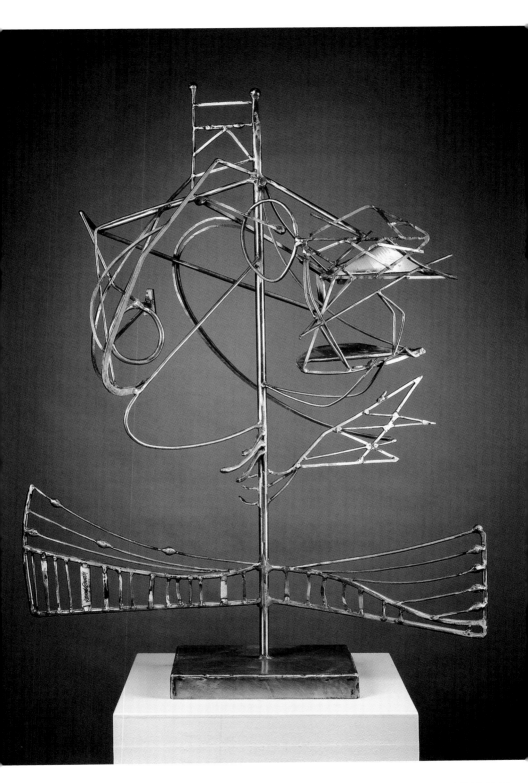

▲ **Willem de Kooning**
American, born the
Netherlands, 1904–1997
Eddy Farm, 1964
Oil on newsprint mounted
on board, 30 x 45 in.
Bequest of Robert H. Halff
© 2010 The Willem de
Kooning Foundation /
Artists Rights Society (ARS),
New York

◀ **Alberto Giacometti**
Swiss, 1901–1966
Bust of Annette IV, 1962
Bronze, 22 ⅞ in. high
Mary and Sylvan Lang Collection
© 2010 Succession Giacometti /
Artists Rights Society (ARS),
New York / ADAGP, Paris

Barbara Hepworth

One of the most represented sculptors in the McNay collection, Barbara Hepworth began as a carver in wood or stone. *Winged Figure II* (1957) comes from the period when she first adopted bronze casting to fulfill public commissions and create editions, or multiple castings, of her works. The McNay is fortunate to have three major bronzes of the late 1950s, as well as a carved and painted wood sculpture of the 1940s and a small bronze of 1958. All exploit the void for expressive effect. *Winged Figure II*, with its two curved and pierced, wing-like planes joined by a web of crossing wires, was made on a larger scale as a commission for the John Lewis Oxford Street department store in London, where it is mounted on a façade high above the street. For many of her bronzes, Hepworth developed unusual surface treatments, such as the applied plaster on the planes of *Winged Figure II*, imparting direct evidence of the artist's hand.

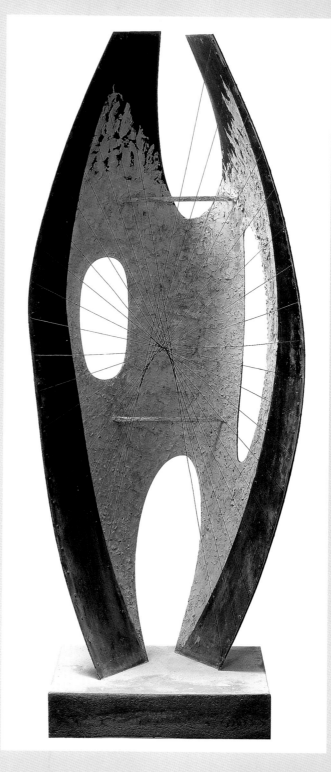

▶ **Barbara Hepworth**
British, 1903–1975
Winged Figure II, 1957
Bronze with plaster and wire,
67⅞ in. high
Gift of the Estate of Tom Slick
© Bowness, Hepworth Estate

◀ **Robert Indiana**
American, born 1928
Decade Autoportrait
1961,1972–77
Oil on canvas, 72 x 72 in.
Gift of Robert L. B. Tobin
© Morgan Art Foundation /
Artists Rights Society (ARS),
New York

◀ **Frederick Hammersley**
American, 1919–2002
Reflect Upon, 1975
Oil on linen, 32 x 32 in.
Gift of the Friends of
the McNay
© Frederick Hammersley
Foundation

Robert Indiana

Widely known for his use of the word *love* as the sole subject of objects in many media, Pop art icon Robert Indiana is well represented at the McNay with paintings, works on paper, and designs for theatre. His *Decade Autoportrait 1961* references the 1960s, with each number, word, and shape signifying an aspect of Indiana's life and ambitions. In this and two other large oils at the McNay—*Leaves* (1965) and *The Metamorphosis of Norma Jean Mortenson* (1967)—the artist used his typical stenciled typography.

On a smaller scale yet exceptionally engaging, Indiana's numerous scene and costume designs for a production of *The Mother of Us All* employ flat graphics and bold colors to visualize the words and music of this Gertrude Stein and Virgil Thomson opera about women's suffrage. Precisely cut from solid colored papers and masterfully collaged to form the opera's scene locations and many characters, the designs transcend their function as guides for the full-scale stage versions. *The Mother of Us All* designs were collected and donated by Robert L. B. Tobin, an important McNay benefactor and friend of Indiana.

▲ **Robert Indiana**
American, born 1928
Scene design for Drawing Room in the House of Susan B. Anthony, Act II, scenes 1 and 2, in *The Mother of Us All*, 1976
Cut paper, 28 ½ x 40 in.
Gift of Robert L. B. Tobin
© Morgan Art Foundation / Artists Rights Society (ARS), New York

Contemporary Art

The McNay's growing collection of contemporary art features a diverse mix of paintings, sculptures, and works on paper that explore the wide range of approaches used by recent artists. With a focus primarily on American artists after 1970, gifts and strategic purchases allow for expanding this area of the collection regularly. The McNay Contemporary Collectors Forum (MCCF), an affiliate membership group, supports annual acquisitions of contemporary art.

The collection has strengths in several late twentieth-century art movements, representing Abstract Expressionist painting and sculpture, geometric abstraction and optical art, and assemblage and minimal sculpture. These unite with recent acquisitions of works based on the human figure, as well as photographic images and installation art.

Pop art paintings by Indiana and a construction by Red Grooms contrast with the repetitive abstractions and optical works by Gene Davis, Valerie Jaudon, Larry Poons, and Julian Stanczak. Ed and Nancy Reddin Kienholz's narrative wall tableau, a group of collages by Robert Motherwell, a Robert Rauschenberg painting with rubbings and collage, and John Chamberlain's wall-mounted assemblage build upon a direction established with Mrs. McNay's bequest of Picasso's 1912 collage, *Guitar and Wine Glass* (p. 26). Leonardo Drew's immense accumulation of salvaged and recycled objects and Chakaia Booker's pedestal sculpture fashioned from black rubber tires join this group of works that recycle manufactured detritus. By way of contrast, Larry Bell, Donald Judd, and Beverly Pepper enhance the collection with elegant minimalist sculptures.

The figure re-emerges in the varied work of sculptors Nicolas Africano and George Segal, as well as the hanging tapestry of Lesley Dill. Robert Morris's large pastel of the early 1980s, with its heavy, deep black plaster-like frame, prefigures the dark mood of the nation post-9/11. An energetic and textured abstraction by painter Sam Gilliam extends the experiments of Washington Color School artists. In Roger Shimomura's self portrait as a Pop art hero, he surrounds himself with myriad cartoon and anime characters easily recognized by the younger generation. Photographs by Ernesto Pujol, Sandy Skoglund, Kathy Vargas, and Massimo Vitali began new directions in collecting for the McNay in the late twentieth and early twenty-first centuries.

◀ **Leonardo Drew**
American, born 1961
Number 33A (detail), 1999
Found objects with wire, tape, and rust,
99 x 114 x 22 in.
Museum purchase with the Helen and Everett H. Jones Purchase Fund

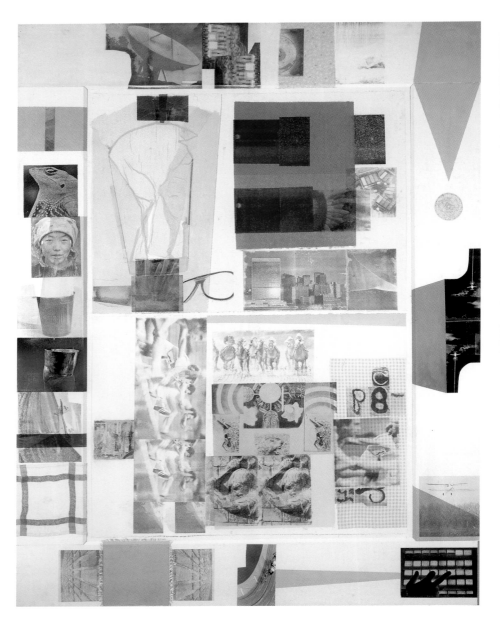

▲ **Robert Rauschenberg**
American, 1925–2008
Rush #5 from the
Cloister Series, 1980
Oil on canvas,
with rubbings and collage,
96 x 72 in.

Gift of Robert H. Halff
Art © Estate of Robert
Rauschenberg / Licensed by
VAGA, New York, NY

▶ Sculpture Gallery
in the Stieren Center
for Exhibitions

Sculpture at top:
Alexander Calder
American, 1898–1976
Four Winds, 1963
Painted steel and aluminum,
76 x 40 x 40 in. at greatest extent
Bequest of Robert H. Halff
© 2010 Calder Foundation, New
York / Artists Rights Society
(ARS), New York

Artists with ties to Texas include John Alexander, whose swamp scene reverberates with creatures of east Texas, and Vernon Fisher of Fort Worth, whose shaped panel simulates a chalkboard with enigmatic white drawings. San Antonio-based artists Carl Embrey, César Martínez, Reginald Rowe, and Kent Rush, each following different paths, are represented in depth. Margo Sawyer's colorful, abstract wall relief and Ray Smith's paintings bordering on magical realism add further variety.

A geometric kinetic work by George Rickey (inside front cover) holds pride of place as the public's favorite among the growing outdoor sculpture collection on the grounds. Referencing the human form are an abstracted head by Tony Cragg, a minimalist figure by Joel Shapiro (inside back cover), and a monumental, stainless steel portrait head by Philip Grausman, commissioned by the McNay.

▶ Donald Judd
American, 1928–1994
Untitled, 1989
Aluminum with Plexiglas,
39 3/8 x 39 3/8 x 19 5/8 in.
Museum purchase with the
Alvin Whitley Fund, with
additional funds from
Ann and Fredrick Erck
Art © Judd Foundation /
Licensed by VAGA,
New York, NY

▶ Julian Stanczak
American, born Poland, 1928
Western Color, 1973
Acrylic on canvas, 48 x 48 in.
Gift of Marianne C. and
Stewart R. Reuter

▲ **Roger Shimomura**
American, born 1939
Him-a-Hero, 2004
Acrylic on canvas, 60 x 72 in.
Museum purchase with funds
from the McNay Contemporary
Collectors Forum

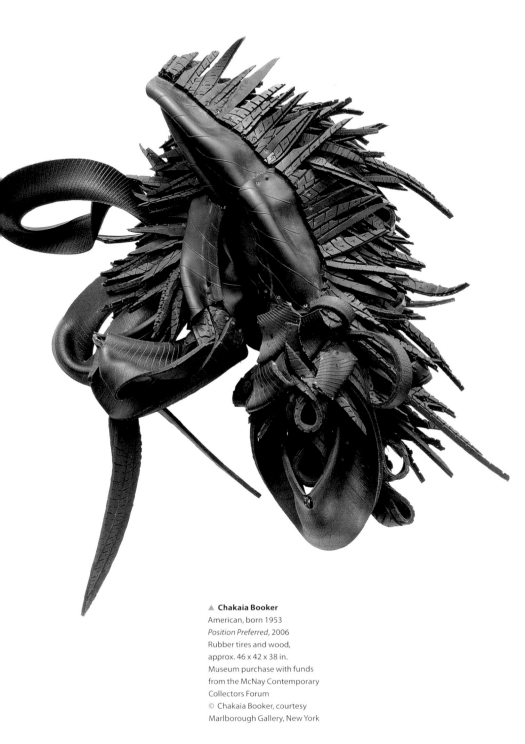

▲ **Chakaia Booker**
American, born 1953
Position Preferred, 2006
Rubber tires and wood,
approx. 46 x 42 x 38 in.
Museum purchase with funds
from the McNay Contemporary
Collectors Forum
© Chakaia Booker, courtesy
Marlborough Gallery, New York

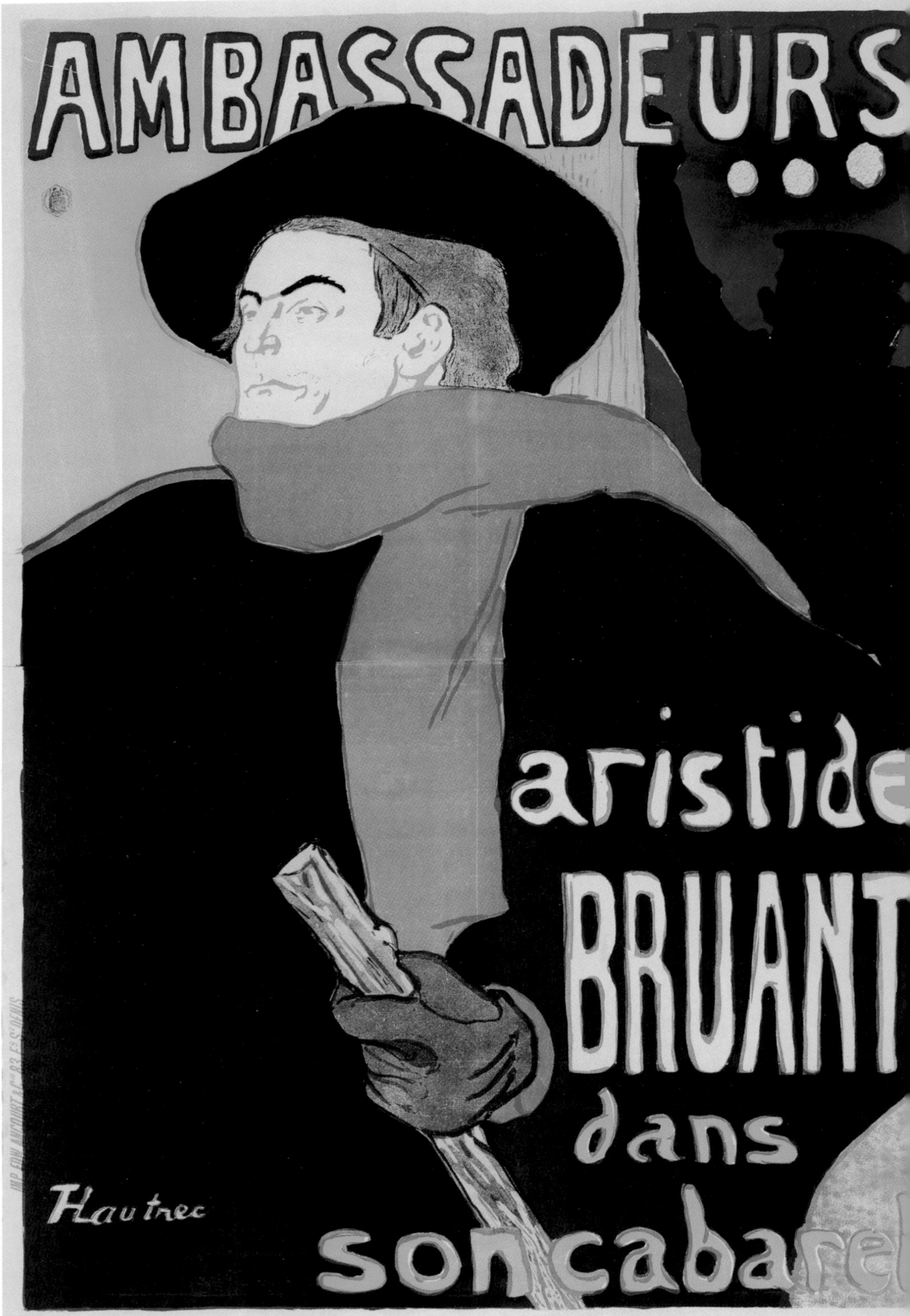
AMBASSADEURS
aristide
BRUANT
dans
son caba

Prints and Drawings

Formed as a complement to the museum's paintings and sculptures, the McNay's print collection is recognized nationally for its focus on the graphics of the nineteenth and twentieth centuries as well as for the overall quality of its holdings. Particular areas of strength are nineteenth-century French and American prints, German Expressionist graphics, and American works on paper of the twentieth and twenty-first centuries—especially post-1960. Graphic media represented include works in relief, intaglio, lithography, screenprinting, drawings, pastels, and watercolors.

While Mrs. McNay's founding bequest included a small number of prints, notably fine etchings by Howard Cook, the museum began systematically acquiring prints to form a cohesive collection in 1960. The Friends of the McNay, founded in 1959, have provided funds to buy more than 500 of the museum's best prints. Other individual donors, including Mary and Sylvan Lang, Jerry Lawson, Margaret Batts Tobin, and Robert L. B. Tobin, greatly enriched the collection with their gifts and bequests.

◀ **Henri de Toulouse-Lautrec**
French, 1864–1901
Aristide Bruant aux Ambassadeurs (detail), 1892
Lithograph, image 53 x 36¾ in.
Mary and Sylvan Lang Collection

▶ **Honoré Daumier**
French, 1808–1879
Rue Transnonain, 1834
Lithograph,
image 11⁵/₁₆ x 17⁷/₁₆ in.
Gift of the Friends of the McNay

The museum has collected the graphics of several artists in considerable depth, including Braque, Cassatt (p. 20), Francisco Goya, Jasper Johns, Matisse, Picasso, and Henri de Toulouse-Lautrec. With a collection exceeding 3,000 prints and 1,500 drawings, pastels, and watercolors, the McNay acquires works on paper on an ongoing basis.

In order to protect works on paper from overexposure to light and humidity, an active schedule of changing exhibitions in the Jerry Lawson Print Gallery and the Charles Butt Paperworks Gallery is the primary means of sharing the McNay's graphic treasures with the public. Of equal importance are Print Room visits by appointment, hosted by the curator of prints and drawings for hundreds of area high school and college students every year. Since true connoisseurship of prints requires that they be seen out of their frames and without a sheet of glass covering them, these visits fulfill an essential function of any print room.

◄ **Erich Heckel**
German, 1883–1970
Portrait of a Man, 1919
Woodcut,
image 18³/₁₆ x 12¾ in.
Gift of the Friends of
the McNay

▶ Jerry Lawson Print Gallery

Jasper Johns

The McNay's long history with Jasper Johns began in 1968, when the museum acquired his *Numerals 0–9* (1968), a suite of ten lithographs. The following year, director John Leeper organized the first retrospective of Johns's prints. The catalogue that Leeper wrote for this landmark show was the first catalogue raisonné of the artist's graphic work. Throughout the 1970s and 1980s, the McNay acquired additional prints by Johns and encouraged others, including Jerry Lawson, to collect his work as well. In her bequest of 1994, Lawson left nineteen of Johns's prints, including the masterpieces *Decoy* (1971), *Decoy II* (1973), and two versions of *Ventriloquist* (1985, 1986).

With thirty-nine prints in the McNay collection, Johns is one of the museum's most fully represented contemporary artists. These works span the artist's career from the 1960s through the 1990s and include many of his greatest prints. One of the incomparable printmakers of the twentieth century, rivaling Picasso in output and influence, Johns considers his prints as important as his paintings and sculptures. The McNay's holdings of these works constitute a highlight of the entire museum collection.

▲ **Jasper Johns**
American, born 1930
Decoy, 1971
Lithograph, sheet 41 x 29 in.

Bequest of Mrs. Jerry Lawson
Art © Jasper Johns / Licensed
by VAGA, New York, NY

Theatre Arts

Founded by San Antonio collector and philanthropist Robert L. B. Tobin, the Tobin Collection of Theatre Arts is one of the finest of its kind in the United States and rivals collections worldwide. With over 10,000 objects, the collection encompasses theatre in Europe and America from 1600 to the present. Devotion to visual artists in the theatre, from Edward Burne-Jones and Edouard Vuillard to Robert Indiana (p. 43) and David Hockney, distinguishes the collection. With individual productions represented in depth, changing installations of the collection often reveal the process through which designers and directors collaborate to give visual form to playwrights' words or composers' music.

Rare books are the collection's historical foundation and hence the Tobin Theatre Arts Gallery was conceived as a grand library. From Greek tragedies to romantic ballets, illustrated books provide records of Western theatre before the twentieth century. The McNay is noted for Renaissance and Baroque festival books, recording courtly ceremonies of the Medici and the Bourbons, and for treatises on

◀ **Guiseppe Bibiena**
Italian, 1696–1756
Scene design for noble
atrium (detail), 1700s
Graphite, ink, and watercolor
on paper, 13 x 9 in.
Gift of the Tobin Endowment

▶ Entrance to Tobin Theatre
Arts Gallery

illusionistic perspective by the Bibiena family and other architects. Since all theatre is ephemeral, books are invaluable to modernism as well, whether theoretical texts by modernist pioneers in Germany or programs for French avant-garde theatres with lithographs by Toulouse-Lautrec.

Plays by William Shakespeare, which continue to inspire visionary designers, digress from the Tobin Collection's emphasis on musical theatre. Edward Gordon Craig's daring and disastrous *Hamlet* at the Moscow Art Theatre (1911) is especially significant. Craig and Robert Edmond Jones, a fellow proponent of the New Stagecraft in England and America, initiated antinaturalistic reforms still important today. Tanya Moiseivitsch's emphasis on the actor on the open or thrust stage at the Stratford Festival in Ontario (built 1953) and Ralph Koltai's search for visual metaphor in his settings for the Royal Shakespeare Company (1976–present) attest to ongoing creative fascination with the Bard.

No performances are more unabashedly theatrical than operas and the Tobin Collection embraces the medium, from Wolfgang Amadeus Mozart, Giuseppe Verdi, and Giacomo Puccini to Benjamin Britten and Philip Glass. Eugene Berman and Timothy O'Brien, active at the Metropolitan Opera and Royal Opera respectively, are among mid to late twentieth-century designers represented in depth. Their work—costume drawings and scenic maquettes (models) for such repertory standards as *Don Giovanni* (1957) and *Turandot* (1983)—demonstrates the monumental task of opera design. Recently acquired maquettes by Adrianne Lobel for John Adams's *Nixon in China* (1987) and by Paul Steinberg for Stewart Wallace's *Harvey Milk* (1995) keep the Tobin Collection up to date in the media age.

Enthusiasts of the American musical may trace its origins to lavishly designed revues at the Ziegfeld Follies and Radio City Music Hall from the 1910s through the 1930s. Post-World War II designers Bill and Jean Eckart, Jo Mielziner, and Oliver Smith put their visual stamp on such Broadway golden age classics as *South Pacific* (1949), *West Side Story* (1957), and *Damn Yankees* (1955). Musicals by Stephen Sondheim stand out in the Tobin Collection, as they have on the stage, beginning with *A Funny Thing Happened on the Way to the Forum* (1962), designed by Tony Walton. Ann Hould-Ward and Tony Straiges bring Post-Impressionist paintings to life in Sondheim's *Sunday in the Park with George* (1984), one of many works linking theatre design with art history.

The Ballets Russes

Sergei Diaghilev's Ballets Russes thrilled audiences with its synthesis of modern painting, music, and choreography. The impact of costumes and scenery manifests itself in the fairytale romanticism of Alexandre Benois's designs for *Giselle* (1910) and the orientalist exoticism of Léon Bakst's *Shéhérazade* (1910), as well as in the folkloric exuberance of Natalia Gontcharova's *Le Coq d'Or* (Production 1914) and the Cubo-Futurist daring of Mikhail Larionov's *Chout* (1921). In his continual quest to surprise, Diaghilev turned to such Paris-based Modernists as Matisse and Picasso, setting the precedent for other artists to venture from studio to stage, including Giorgio de Chirico, Sonia Delaunay, Alexandra Exter, Léger, Joan Miró, and László Moholy-Nagy.

▲ **Léon Bakst**
Russian, 1866–1924
Costume design for Vaslav
Nijinsky as Chinese Dancer in
Les Orientales, 1917

Watercolor and graphite
on paper, 18 x 25⅜ in.
Gift of the Tobin Foundation

◀ **Edward Gordon Craig**
British, 1872–1966
Scene design for Hamlet
Greeting the Actors, Act III in
Hamlet, 1926
Watercolor and pastel on
paper, 18 x 22½ in.
Gift of Margaret Batts Tobin

▲ **Ralph Koltai**
British, born Germany, 1924
Maquette for a Royal
National Theatre
production of *Richard III*,
ca. 1979
Lead, wood, and painted
metal, 10¼ x 19¼ x 19 in.
Gift of the Tobin Endowment

▶ **Eugene Berman**
American, born Russia,
1899–1972
Costume design for Don
Pedro, Il Commendatore,
from *Don Giovanni*, 1957
Watercolor and ink on paper,
9¹³/₁₆ x 7 in.
Gift of the Tobin Endowment

Medieval and Renaissance Art

In 1955, Dr. and Mrs. Frederic Oppenheimer, friends of Mrs. McNay, gave to the museum their collection of medieval and Renaissance sculptures and paintings, which they had been forming since the 1920s. The paintings, primarily altarpiece fragments and portraits, include notable works by Albrecht Bouts, the Master of Frankfurt, and Jan Gossaert (called Mabuse) among the Northern masters; and Taddeo di Bartolo and Alvise Vivarini among the Italian school artists. Sculptures in the Oppenheimer collection several of which are parts of larger works or ensembles, are French, German, or Netherlandish. Installed in three rooms on the second floor of the museum, the Oppenheimer collection provides a fascinating parallel to the religious art of New Mexico collected by Mrs. McNay.

▲ **Albrecht Bouts**
Netherlandish,
ca. 1452–1549
Moses and the Burning Bush
and *Gideon and
the Fleece*, ca. 1490
Oil on panels, 27¾ x 8 in.
and 27¾ x 8¼ in.
Gifts of Dr. and Mrs.
Frederic G. Oppenheimer

▶ Medieval and
Renaissance Art in the
Oppenheimer Galleries

▲ Art from New Mexico
in the Hamon Galleries

▶ **New Mexico**
San Miguel Arcángel
(St. Michael the
Archangel), ca. 1860
Wood with water-
soluble paint, string,
and tin, 20 ⅛ in. high
Bequest of Marion
Koogler McNay

Art of New Mexico

On summer visits to New Mexico, Mrs. McNay
amassed a large collection of Native American and
New Mexican folk art. She acquired several dozen
santos—both *retablos* (paintings) and *bultos*
(sculptures)—when Catholic churches in New
Mexico replaced their folk art masterpieces with
store-bought church art. These simple yet powerful
works suited her taste for bold color and form, and
their roughhewn naïve character answered her
love for seeing the artist's hand at work. Mrs.
McNay also obtained fine collections of Rio Grande
blankets, ceramics, jewelry, furniture, and paintings
by the American Indian school established by
Dorothy Dunn, as well as watercolors by members
of the Taos Society of Artists.

Complementing Mrs. McNay's works is an
exceptional group of *kachina* dolls given by Jane
Stieren Lacy. The skills for creating these figures,
which symbolize the spiritual beings of the Pueblo
people, transferred easily to Spanish saint-makers
who carved *bultos* for the mission churches.

First published in 2010 by
Scala Publishers Ltd
Northburgh House
10 Northburgh Street
London EC1V 0AT
Telephone: +44 (0) 20 7490 9900
www.scalapublishers.com

In association with
McNay Art Museum
6000 North New Braunfels
Post Office Box 6069
San Antonio, Texas 78209-0069
www.mcnayart.org

British Library Cataloguing in Publication Data.
A catalogue record for this book is available
from the British Library.

ISBN: 978 1 85759 664 9 (Scala)
ISBN: 978 0 916677 54 1 (McNay)

For the McNay
Compiler and Editor: Rose M. Glennon

For Scala
Project Manager and Copy Editor: Linda Schofield
Designer: Nigel Soper

Diagrams: p. 15: Jessica Haynes, Soleil Advertising

Photography: pp. 16 (top and bottom), 17 (center),
47, inside back cover: © Jeff Goldberg / ESTO
P. 14: © 1996 Hester + Hardaway
P. 62 (top): Robert LaPrelle, Kimbell Art Museum
Pp. 6, 8, 9, 10, 11, 12, 13 (top and bottom): McNay Art
Museum Library and Archives
All other photographs: Michael J. Smith

Printed and bound in Singapore

10 9 8 7 6 5 4 3 2 1

Library of Congress Cataloging-in-Publication Data

McNay Art Museum.
    McNay Art Museum : an introduction. – 1st ed.
      p. cm.
    ISBN 978-0-916677-54-1 (pbk. : alk. paper)
1. McNay Art Museum. 2. Art–Texas–San Antonio.
I. Title.
    N736.A85 2010
    708.164'351–dc22
                        2010020145